contents

D1299301

7

26

51

54

Chicken & Turkey

Picante Skillet Chicken

Makes 6 servings

PREP TIME
5 minutes

COOK TIME
20 minutes

1 tablespoon vegetable oil

6 skinless, boneless chicken breast halves (about 1½ pounds)

1 jar (16 ounces) Pace® Picante Sauce

6 cups hot cooked rice

1. Heat the oil in a 10-inch skillet over medium-high heat. Add the chicken and cook for 10 minutes or until well browned on both sides.

2. Stir the picante sauce in the skillet and heat to a boil. Reduce the heat to medium. Cover and cook for 5 minutes or until the chicken is cooked through. Serve the chicken and sauce with the rice.

Quick Chicken Parmesan

Makes 4 servings

PREP TIME
5 minutes

BAKE TIME
25 minutes

4 skinless, boneless chicken breast halves (about 1 pound)

2 cups Prego® Traditional Italian Sauce *or* Fresh Mushroom Italian Sauce

2 ounces shredded mozzarella cheese (about ½ cup)

2 tablespoons grated Parmesan cheese

½ of a 16-ounce package spaghetti, cooked and drained (about 4 cups)

1. Place the chicken in a 2-quart shallow baking dish. Top the chicken with the Italian sauce. Sprinkle with the mozzarella cheese and Parmesan cheese.

2. Bake at 400°F. for 25 minutes or until cooked through. Serve with the spaghetti.

Creamy Chicken Dijon

Makes 4 servings

1 tablespoon vegetable oil

4 skinless, boneless chicken breast halves (about 1 pound)

1 can (10¾ ounces) Campbell's® Condensed Cream of Chicken Soup (Regular *or* 98% Fat Free)

½ cup water

1 tablespoon coarse-grain Dijon-style mustard

1 tablespoon dry white wine

1 teaspoon dried parsley flakes

1 teaspoon packed brown sugar

½ teaspoon onion powder

¼ teaspoon dried tarragon leaves, crushed

Dash garlic powder

PREP TIME
10 minutes

COOK TIME
20 minutes

1. Heat the oil in a 10-inch skillet over medium-high heat. Add the chicken and cook for 10 minutes or until well browned on both sides.

2. Stir the soup, water, mustard, wine, parsley, brown sugar, onion powder, tarragon and garlic powder in the skillet and heat to a boil. Reduce the heat to low. Cover and cook for 5 minutes or until the chicken is cooked through.

Creamy Mushroom-Garlic Chicken

Makes 4 servings

PREP TIME
5 minutes

COOK TIME
20 minutes

1 tablespoon vegetable oil

4 skinless, boneless chicken breast halves (about 1 pound)

1 can (10¾ ounces) Campbell's® Condensed Cream of Mushroom with Roasted Garlic Soup

½ cup milk

1. Heat the oil in a 10-inch skillet over medium-high heat. Add the chicken and cook for 10 minutes or until well browned on both sides.

2. Stir the soup and milk in the skillet and heat to a boil. Reduce the heat to low. Cover and cook for 5 minutes or until the chicken is cooked through.

For Creamy Herbed Chicken: Substitute Campbell's® Condensed Cream of Chicken with Herbs Soup for the Cream of Mushroom with Roasted Garlic.

Turkey & Broccoli Alfredo

Makes 4 servings

- ½ package (8 ounces) linguine
- 1 cup fresh *or* frozen broccoli florets
- 1 can (10¾ ounces) Campbell's® Condensed Cream of Mushroom Soup (Regular *or* 98% Fat Free)
- ½ cup milk
- ½ cup grated Parmesan cheese
- ¼ teaspoon ground black pepper
- 2 cups cubed cooked turkey

PREP TIME
10 minutes

COOK TIME
20 minutes

1. Prepare the linguine according to the package directions in a 3-quart saucepan. Add the broccoli during the last 4 minutes of the cooking time. Drain the linguine mixture well in a colander. Return the linguine mixture to the saucepan.

2. Stir the soup, milk, cheese, black pepper and turkey in the saucepan and cook over medium heat until the mixture is hot and bubbling, stirring occasionally. Serve with additional Parmesan cheese.

Serving Suggestion: Serve with a Caesar salad. For dessert, serve your favorite fresh fruit.

Kitchen **Tip**

Substitute spaghetti for the linguine.

Crunchy Chicken and Gravy

Makes 4 servings

PREP TIME
10 minutes

BAKE TIME
20 minutes

COOK TIME
5 minutes

1 cup Pepperidge Farm® Herb Seasoned Stuffing, crushed

2 tablespoons grated Parmesan cheese

1 egg

4 skinless, boneless chicken breast halves (about 1 pound)

2 tablespoons butter, melted

1 jar (12 ounces) Campbell's® Slow Roast Chicken Gravy

1. Stir the stuffing and cheese on a plate. Beat the egg in a shallow dish with a fork or whisk. Dip the chicken into the egg. Coat the chicken with the stuffing mixture. Place the chicken onto a baking sheet. Drizzle with the butter.

2. Bake at 400°F. for 20 minutes or until the chicken is cooked through.

3. Heat the gravy in a 1-quart saucepan over medium heat until hot and bubbling. Serve the gravy with the chicken.

Southwest Salsa Chicken with Fresh Greens

Makes 6 servings

1 tablespoon chili powder

1 teaspoon ground cumin

6 skinless, boneless chicken breasts (about 1½ pounds), cut into strips

1 tablespoon olive oil

1 cup Pace® Picante Sauce

¼ cup water

1 bag (about 7 ounces) mixed salad greens

PREP TIME
10 minutes

COOK TIME
20 minutes

1. Stir the chili powder and cumin in a medium bowl. Add the chicken and toss to coat.

2. Heat the oil in a 12-inch skillet over medium-high heat. Add the chicken and cook for 15 minutes or until well browned and cooked through, stirring often. Remove the chicken from the skillet, cover and keep warm.

3. Stir the picante sauce and water in the skillet and cook until the mixture is hot and bubbling. Divide the greens among **6** plates. Top with the chicken and sauce mixture.

Turkey Broccoli Divan

Makes 4 servings

PREP TIME
10 minutes

COOK TIME
20 minutes

4 cups cooked broccoli florets

1½ cups cubed cooked turkey

1 can (10¾ ounces) Campbell's® Condensed Cream of Chicken Soup (Regular *or* 98% Fat Free)

⅓ cup milk

½ cup shredded Cheddar cheese

2 tablespoons dry bread crumbs

1 tablespoon butter, melted

1. Place the broccoli and turkey into a 9-inch pie plate.

2. Stir the soup and milk in a small bowl. Pour the soup mixture over the turkey and broccoli. Top with the cheese.

3. Stir the bread crumbs and butter in a small bowl. Sprinkle over the cheese.

4. Bake at 450°F. for 20 minutes or until the mixture is hot and bubbling.

Serving Suggestion: Serve with a cucumber and tomato salad topped with red wine vinaigrette. For dessert serve a fresh citrus fruit cup (orange, grapefruit and tangerine sections) drizzled with honey and a sprig of fresh mint.

Barbecued Chicken Sandwiches

Makes 4 servings

1 tablespoon butter

1 small green pepper, chopped (about ½ cup) (optional)

1 small onion, chopped (about ¼ cup)

¼ cup chopped celery

½ cup barbecue sauce

2 cans (4.5 ounces *each*) Swanson® Premium White Chunk Chicken Breast in Water, drained

4 Pepperidge Farm® Classic Sandwich Buns with Sesame Seeds, split and toasted

PREP TIME
10 minutes

COOK TIME
15 minutes

1. Heat the butter in a 2-quart saucepan over medium heat. Stir the green pepper, onion and celery in the saucepan and cook until tender.

2. Stir the barbecue sauce and chicken in the saucepan. Heat until the mixture is hot and bubbling. Divide the chicken mixture among the buns.

Cheesy Chicken Pizza

Makes 4 servings

PREP TIME
15 minutes

BAKE TIME
15 minutes

1 package (about 13 ounces) refrigerated pizza dough

½ cup Pace® Picante Sauce

½ cup Prego® Traditional Italian Sauce *or* Roasted Garlic & Herb Italian Sauce

1 cup chopped cooked chicken *or* turkey

½ cup sliced pitted ripe olives

2 green onions, sliced (about ¼ cup)

4 ounces shredded mozzarella cheese (about 1 cup)

1. Heat the oven to 425°F.

2. Unroll the dough onto a greased 12-inch pizza pan. Press the dough into a 12-inch circle. Pinch up the edge to form a rim.

3. Stir the picante sauce and Italian sauce in a small bowl. Spread the picante sauce mixture over the crust to the rim. Top with the chicken, olives, onions and cheese.

4. Bake for 15 minutes or until the cheese is melted and the crust is golden brown.

Kitchen Tip

For a crispier crust, prepare the dough as directed in step 2. Bake the dough for 5 minutes. Remove the dough from the oven and proceed as directed in steps 3 and 4.

Quick & Easy Chicken Quesadillas

Makes 8 servings

4 skinless, boneless chicken breast halves (about 1 pound), cut into cubes

1 can (10¾ ounces) Campbell's® Condensed Cream of Chicken Soup (Regular *or* 98% Fat Free)

½ cup Pace® Picante Sauce

½ cup shredded Monterey Jack cheese

1 teaspoon chili powder

8 flour tortillas (8-inch), warmed

PREP TIME
15 minutes

COOK TIME
15 minutes

BAKE TIME
5 minutes

1. Heat the oven to 425°F.

2. Cook the chicken in a 10-inch nonstick skillet over medium-high heat until well browned and cooked through, stirring often. Stir in the soup, picante sauce, cheese and chili powder and cook until the mixture is hot and bubbling.

3. Place the tortillas onto **2** baking sheets. Spread **about ⅓ cup** chicken mixture on **half** of **each** tortilla to within ½ inch of the edge. Brush the edges of the tortillas with water. Fold the tortillas over the filling and press the edges to seal.

4. Bake for 5 minutes or until the filling is hot. Cut the quesadillas into wedges.

Turkey Fajitas

Makes 6 servings

PREP TIME
20 minutes

COOK TIME
15 minutes

2 jars (12 ounces ***each***) Franco-American® Slow Roast Turkey Gravy

1 cup Pace® Picante Sauce

2 tablespoons vegetable oil

2 small green ***or*** red peppers, cut into 2-inch-long strips (about 2 cups)

2 medium onions, sliced (about 2 cups)

3 cups cooked turkey ***or*** chicken strips

12 flour tortillas (6-inch), warmed

Sliced pitted ripe olives

Kitchen **Tip**

You can also use cooked steak strips and substitute beef gravy for the turkey gravy.

1. Stir the gravy and picante sauce in a 3-quart saucepan.

2. Heat the oil in a 10-inch skillet over medium heat. Add the peppers and onions and cook until tender-crisp, stirring occasionally. Stir in **2 cups** gravy mixture and the turkey. Reduce the heat to low. Cook until the mixture is hot and bubbling.

3. Spoon ⅓ **cup** turkey mixture down the center of **each** tortilla. Fold the tortillas around the filling. Heat the remaining gravy mixture over medium heat until the mixture is hot and bubbling. Serve with the filled tortillas. Garnish with the olives.

Chicken & Stir-Fry Vegetable Pizza

Makes 4 servings

1 can (10¾ ounces) Campbell's® Condensed Cream of Mushroom Soup (Regular *or* 98% Fat Free)

1 prepared pizza crust (12-inch)

1 tablespoon vegetable oil

3 cups frozen vegetables

⅛ teaspoon garlic powder

1 package (about 10 ounces) refrigerated cooked chicken strips

1 cup shredded Cheddar cheese (about 4 ounces)

Dried oregano leaves *or* crushed red pepper

PREP TIME
5 minutes

COOK TIME
5 minutes

BAKE TIME
10 minutes

1. Spread the soup on the crust to within ¼ inch of the edge. Bake at 450°F. for 5 minutes.

2. Heat the oil in a 10-inch skillet over medium heat. Add the vegetables and garlic powder and cook until the vegetables are tender-crisp, stirring occasionally.

3. Spoon the vegetables on the pizza crust. Top with the chicken and cheese. Sprinkle with the oregano, if desired.

Beef & Pork

Creamy Pork Marsala with Fettuccine

Makes 4 servings

PREP TIME
5 minutes

COOK TIME
25 minutes

Kitchen **Tip**

Marsalas can range from dry to sweet, so be sure to use a dry one for this recipe.

1 tablespoon olive oil

4 boneless pork chops, ¾-inch thick (about 1 pound)

1 cup sliced mushrooms (about 3 ounces)

1 clove garlic, minced

1 can (10¾ ounces) Campbell's® Condensed Cream of Mushroom Soup (Regular *or* 98% Fat Free)

½ cup milk

2 tablespoons dry Marsala wine

8 ounces spinach fettuccine, cooked and drained

1. Heat the oil in a 10-inch skillet over medium-high heat. Add the pork and cook until well browned on both sides.

2. Reduce the heat to medium. Add the mushrooms and garlic to the skillet and cook until the mushrooms are tender.

3. Stir the soup, milk and wine in the skillet and heat to a boil. Reduce the heat to low. Cover and cook for 5 minutes or until the pork is cooked through. Serve the pork and sauce with the pasta.

Zesty Pork Chops

Makes 4 servings

PREP TIME
5 minutes

COOK TIME
30 minute

4 **bone-in pork chops (about 1¼ pounds)**
  All-purpose flour
1 **cup Pace® Picante Sauce**
2 **tablespoons packed brown sugar**
1 **apple, peeled and cut into ¼-inch-thick slices**
2 **tablespoons olive oil**

1. Coat the pork with the flour. Stir the picante sauce, brown sugar and apple in a medium bowl.

2. Heat the oil in a 10-inch skillet over medium-high heat. Add the pork and cook until well browned on both sides. Pour off any fat.

3. Pour the picante sauce mixture over the pork. Reduce the heat to low. Cover and cook for 20 minutes or until the pork is cooked through.

Kitchen Tip

You can really spice up this recipe by adding **1 teaspoon** *hot pepper sauce to the picante sauce mixture.*

Bistro Onion Burgers

Makes 6 servings

1½ pounds ground beef

1 envelope (about 1 ounce) dry onion soup and recipe mix

3 tablespoons water

6 Pepperidge Farm® Classic Sandwich Buns with Sesame Seeds, split and toasted

Lettuce leaves

Tomato slices

PREP TIME
5 minutes

COOK TIME
10 minutes

1. Thoroughly mix the beef, soup mix and water. Shape the beef mixture into **6** (½-inch-thick) burgers.

2. Cook the burgers in batches in a 10-inch skillet over medium-high heat until well browned on both sides, 10 minutes for medium or to desired doneness.

3. Serve the burgers on the buns. Top with the lettuce and tomato.

Steak with Chipotle Cheese Sauce

Makes 8 servings

PREP TIME
20 minutes

COOK TIME
10 minutes

GRILL TIME
15 minutes

1 tablespoon olive oil

2 large white onions *or* 1 large sweet onion, coarsely chopped (about 2 cups)

1 can (10¾ ounces) Campbell's® Condensed Cheddar Cheese Soup

½ cup milk

½ teaspoon ground chipotle chile pepper

2 medium tomatoes, coarsely chopped (about 2 cups)

1 skirt *or* beef flank steak (about 2 pounds), 1-inch thick, cut into 8 pieces

¼ cup chopped fresh cilantro leaves (optional)

1. Heat the oil in a 2-quart saucepan over medium heat. Add the onions and cook for 5 minutes or until tender, stirring occasionally.

2. Stir the soup, milk, chipotle chile pepper and tomatoes in the saucepan. Reduce the heat to low. Cook and stir for 3 minutes or until the mixture is hot and bubbling, stirring occasionally.

3. Lightly oil the grill rack and heat the grill to medium. Grill the beef for 15 minutes for medium or to desired doneness, turning the beef over once halfway through the grilling time. Spoon the soup mixture over the beef and sprinkle with the cilantro, if desired.

Baked Potatoes Olé

Makes 4 servings

1 pound ground beef

1 tablespoon chili powder

1 cup Pace® Picante Sauce

4 hot baked potatoes, split

　Shredded Cheddar cheese

1. Cook the beef and chili powder in a 10-inch skillet over medium-high heat until the beef is well browned, stirring often to separate the meat. Pour off any fat.

2. Stir the picante sauce in the skillet. Reduce the heat to low. Cook until the mixture is hot and bubbling. Serve the beef mixture over the potatoes. Top with the cheese.

PREP TIME
　5 minutes

COOK TIME
　15 minutes

Kitchen **Tip**

To bake the potatoes, pierce the potatoes with a fork. Bake at 400°F. for 1 hour or microwave on HIGH for 12 minutes or until fork-tender.

Pork Tenderloin with Peach & Pecan Sauce

Makes 4 servings

PREP TIME
20 minutes

COOK TIME
20 minutes

1 tablespoon olive oil

1 pork tenderloin (about 1 pound), cut into ¾-inch-thick slices

2 cloves garlic, minced

2 green onions, sliced (about ¼ cup)

1 can (10¾ ounces) Campbell's® Condensed Golden Mushroom Soup

1 can (about 15 ounces) sliced peaches in juice, drained, reserving juice

3 tablespoons low-sodium soy sauce

2 tablespoons honey

¼ cup pecan halves, toasted and broken into large pieces

Hot cooked rice

1. Heat the oil in a 10-inch skillet over medium-high heat. Add the pork and cook until well browned on both sides. Remove the pork from the skillet.

2. Add the garlic and onions to the skillet and cook and stir for 1 minute. Stir the soup, peach juice, soy sauce and honey in the skillet and heat to a boil. Cook for 5 minutes or until the soup mixture is slightly reduced.

3. Return the pork to the skillet. Stir in the peaches. Reduce the heat to low. Cook until the pork is cooked through. Stir in the pecans. Serve the pork and sauce with the rice. Sprinkle with additional sliced green onion, if desired.

Tasty 2-Step Pork Chops

Makes 4 servings

1 tablespoon vegetable oil

4 bone-in pork chops, ½-inch thick (about 1½ pounds)

1 can (10¾ ounces) Campbell's® Condensed Cream of Mushroom Soup (Regular *or* 98% Fat Free)

½ cup water

1. Heat the oil in a 10-inch skillet over medium-high heat. Add the pork and cook until well browned on both sides.

2. Stir the soup and water in the skillet and heat to a boil. Reduce the heat to low. Cover and cook for 10 minutes or until the pork is cooked through.

Garlic Pork Chops: Add **1** clove garlic, minced, to the skillet with the pork chops.

PREP TIME
5 minutes

COOK TIME
20 minutes

Kitchen **Tip**

Also great with Campbell's® Condensed Cream of Mushroom with Roasted Garlic Soup, with ½ cup milk instead of water.

Orange Beef Steak

Makes 6 servings

PREP TIME
10 minutes

COOK TIME
25 minutes

1 jar (12 ounces) Campbell's® Slow Roast Beef Gravy

1 tablespoon grated orange zest

2 tablespoons orange juice

½ teaspoon garlic powder *or* 2 cloves garlic, minced

1 boneless beef top round steak, 1½-inch thick (about 1½ pounds)

1. Stir the gravy, orange zest, orange juice and garlic powder in a 1-quart saucepan.

2. Heat the broiler. Place the beef on a rack in a broiler pan. Broil 4 inches from the heat for 25 minutes for medium or to desired doneness, turning the beef over halfway through cooking and brushing often with the gravy mixture. Thinly slice the beef.

3. Heat the remaining gravy mixture over medium-high heat to a boil. Serve the gravy mixture with the beef.

Soft Tacos

Makes 8 servings

1 pound ground beef

1 package (about 1 ounce) taco seasoning mix

¾ cup water

8 flour tortillas (8-inch), warmed

1 cup Pace® Picante Sauce

1 cup shredded lettuce

1 cup shredded Cheddar cheese

PREP TIME
10 minutes

COOK TIME
15 minutes

1. Cook the beef in a 10-inch skillet over medium-high heat until the beef is well browned, stirring frequently to separate the meat. Pour off any fat.

2. Stir the taco seasoning mix and water in the skillet and heat to a boil. Reduce the heat to low and cook for 5 minutes, stirring occasionally.

3. Spoon **about ¼ cup** beef mixture down the center of **each** tortilla. Top **each** with **about 2 tablespoons** picante sauce, lettuce and cheese. Fold the tortilla around the filling. Serve with additional picante sauce.

Buffalo Burgers

Makes 4 servings

PREP TIME
10 minutes

GRILL TIME
10 minutes

COOK TIME
10 minutes

1 pound ground beef

1 can (10¾ ounces) Campbell's® Condensed Tomato Soup (Regular *or* Healthy Request®)

½ teaspoon Louisiana-style hot sauce

½ cup crumbled blue cheese *or* 4 slices blue cheese

4 Pepperidge Farm® Sandwich Buns with Sesame Seeds, split Lettuce leaves, red onion slices, tomato slices (optional)

1. Shape the beef into **4** (½-inch-thick) burgers.

2. Lightly oil the grill rack and heat the grill to medium. Grill the burgers for 10 minutes for medium or to desired doneness, turning the burgers over once halfway through the grilling time.

3. Heat the soup and hot sauce in a 1-quart saucepan over medium heat to a boil. Reduce the heat to low. Cover and cook for 5 minutes. Top the burgers with the soup mixture. Sprinkle with the cheese. Serve the burgers on the buns with the lettuce, onion and tomato, if desired.

Serving Suggestion: Serve with carrot and celery sticks with ranch dressing for dipping. For dessert, serve chocolate chip cookies topped with vanilla ice cream.

Kitchen **Tip**

Any leftover soup mixture can also be a great dipping sauce for French fries.

Shortcut Stuffed Peppers

Makes 4 servings

1½ **pounds ground beef**

1 **can (10¾ ounces) Campbell's® Condensed Tomato Soup**

1 **cup *uncooked* instant white rice**

2 **teaspoons garlic powder**

½ **teaspoon ground black pepper**

2 **large green peppers, cut in half lengthwise and seeded**

1. Mix the beef, soup, rice, garlic powder and black pepper in a large bowl.

2. Place the pepper halves, cut-side up, into an 8×8-inch microwavable baking dish. Divide the beef mixture among the pepper halves (the pepper halves will be very full).

3. Cover and microwave on HIGH for 10 minutes or until the beef mixture is cooked through.

PREP TIME
10 minutes

COOK TIME
10 minutes

Kitchen **Tip**

The shortcut is in the cooking— arrange the peppers in the glass dish in a circle for the most effective cooking in the microwave.

Mushroom-Smothered Beef Burgers

Makes 4 servings

PREP TIME
15 minutes

COOK TIME
25 minutes

1 can (10¾ ounces) Campbell's® Condensed Cream of Mushroom Soup (Regular *or* 98% Fat Free)

1 pound ground beef

⅓ cup Italian-seasoned dry bread crumbs

1 small onion, finely chopped (about ¼ cup)

1 egg, beaten

1 tablespoon vegetable oil

1 tablespoon Worcestershire sauce

2 tablespoons water

1½ cups sliced mushrooms (about 4 ounces)

Kitchen Tip

You can substitute ground turkey for the ground beef in this recipe.

1. Thoroughly mix ¼ **cup** soup, beef, bread crumbs, onion and egg in a large bowl. Shape the beef mixture **firmly** into **4** (½-inch-thick) burgers.

2. Heat the oil in a 10-inch skillet over medium-high heat. Add the burgers and cook until they're well browned on both sides. Pour off any fat.

3. Add the remaining soup, Worcestershire, water and mushrooms to the skillet and heat to a boil. Reduce the heat to low. Cover and cook for 10 minutes or until the burgers are cooked through.

Quick Spaghetti & Meatballs

Makes 6 servings

1 jar (45 ounces) Prego® Flavored with Meat Italian Sauce

16 frozen meatballs (1 ounce *each)*

1 package (1 pound) spaghetti, cooked and drained (about 8 cups)

Grated Parmesan cheese

PREP TIME
5 minutes

COOK TIME
25 minutes

1. Stir the Italian sauce and meatballs in a 3-quart saucepan and heat to a boil over medium heat. Reduce the heat to low. Cover and cook for 20 minutes or until the meatballs are heated through, stirring occasionally.

2. Serve the sauce and meatballs over the spaghetti. Sprinkle with the cheese.

Steak with Tomato Gorgonzola Sauce

Makes 6 servings

PREP TIME
10 minutes

COOK TIME
25 minutes

Vegetable cooking spray

1 boneless beef sirloin steak *or* top round steak, ¾-inch thick, thinly sliced (about 1½ pounds)

1 package (8 ounces) sliced mushrooms

1 large onion, thinly sliced (about 1 cup)

¼ cup balsamic vinegar

1 cup Prego® Traditional Italian Sauce *or* Marinara Italian Sauce

½ cup crumbled gorgonzola *or* feta cheese

Hot mashed potatoes

1. Spray a 12-inch skillet with the cooking spray and heat over medium-high heat for 1 minute. Add the beef in 2 batches and cook until well browned, stirring often. Remove the beef from the skillet. Pour off any fat.

2. Reduce the heat to medium. Add the mushrooms and onion to the skillet and cook for 5 minutes or until the vegetables are tender. Stir in the vinegar and cook for 2 minutes.

3. Stir the Italian sauce in the skillet and heat to a boil. Return the beef to the skillet. Top with the cheese. Cook and stir until the cheese is melted. Serve with the potatoes.

Polynesian Burgers

Makes 6 servings

1½ pounds ground beef

  1 can (8 ounces) pineapple slices in juice, undrained

  1 can (10½ ounces) Campbell's® Condensed French Onion Soup

  2 teaspoons packed brown sugar

  1 tablespoon cider vinegar

  1 loaf French bread, cut crosswise into 6 pieces

PREP TIME
10 minutes

COOK TIME
20 minutes

1. Shape the beef into **6** (½-inch-thick) burgers.

2. Cook the burgers in a 12-inch skillet over medium-high heat until well browned on both sides. Pour off any fat. Top **each** burger with **1** slice pineapple. Reserve the pineapple juice.

3. Stir the soup, reserved pineapple juice, brown sugar and vinegar in a small bowl. Add the soup mixture to the skillet and heat to a boil. Reduce the heat to low. Cover and cook for 5 minutes or until the burgers are cooked through.

4. Split the bread pieces. Serve the burgers and sauce on the bread.

Pork with Mushroom Dijon Sauce

Makes 4 servings

PREP TIME
10 minutes

COOK TIME
30 minutes

4 boneless pork chops, ¾-inch thick (about 1 pound)

½ teaspoon lemon pepper seasoning

1 tablespoon vegetable oil

1 cup sliced mushrooms (about 3 ounces)

1 can (10¾ ounces) Campbell's® Condensed Cream of Mushroom Soup (Regular *or* 98% Fat Free)

¼ cup milk

2 tablespoons Chablis *or* other dry white wine

1 tablespoon Dijon-style mustard

1. Season the pork with the lemon pepper.

2. Heat the oil in a 10-inch skillet over medium-high heat. Add the pork and cook until well browned on both sides. Remove the pork from the skillet.

3. Add the mushrooms to the skillet. Reduce the heat to medium. Cook until the mushrooms are tender, stirring occasionally.

4. Stir the soup, milk, wine and mustard in the skillet and heat to a boil. Return the pork to the skillet. Reduce the heat to low. Cover and cook for 10 minutes or until the pork is cooked through.

Shortcut Ravioli Lasagna

Makes 6 servings

Vegetable cooking spray

3 cups Prego® Italian Sausage & Garlic Italian Sauce

½ cup water

1 package (30 ounces) frozen regular-size cheese-filled ravioli (about 30 to 34)

6 ounces shredded mozzarella cheese (about 1½ cups)

Grated Parmesan cheese *and* chopped fresh parsley for garnish

PREP TIME
10 minutes

BAKE TIME
45 minutes

STAND TIME
10 minutes

1. Heat the oven to 375°F. Spray a 13×9×2-inch baking dish with cooking spray.

2. Stir the Italian sauce and water in a large bowl. Spread **1 cup** of the Italian sauce mixture in the baking dish. Top with ½ of the ravioli, ¾ **cup** mozzarella cheese and **1 cup** sauce mixture. Top with the remaining ravioli and sauce mixture. Cover the baking dish.

3. Bake for 35 minutes or until the mixture is hot and bubbling. Uncover the baking dish. Sprinkle with the remaining mozzarella cheese.

4. Bake for 10 minutes or until the cheese is melted. Let stand for 10 minutes. Garnish with the Parmesan cheese and parsley.

Oodles of Noodles

Three Cheese Baked Ziti with Spinach

Makes 6 servings

PREP TIME
15 minutes

BAKE TIME
30 minutes

1 package (16 ounces) *uncooked* medium tube-shaped pasta (ziti)

1 bag (6 ounces) baby spinach, washed (about 4 cups)

1 jar (1 pound 7 ounces) Prego® Marinara Italian Sauce

1 cup ricotta cheese

4 ounces shredded mozzarella cheese (about 1 cup)

¾ cup grated Parmesan cheese

½ teaspoon garlic powder

¼ teaspoon ground black pepper

1. Prepare the pasta according to the package directions. Add the spinach during the last minute of the cooking time. Drain the pasta and spinach well in a colander. Return them to the saucepot.

2. Stir the Italian sauce, ricotta, ½ **cup** of the mozzarella cheese, ½ **cup** of the Parmesan cheese, garlic powder and black pepper into the pasta mixture. Spoon the pasta mixture into a 13×9×2-inch shallow baking dish. Sprinkle with the remaining mozzarella and Parmesan cheeses.

3. Bake at 350°F. for 30 minutes or until the mixture is hot and bubbling.

Lasagna Roll-Ups

Makes 4 servings

PREP TIME
30 minutes

BAKE TIME
35 minutes

STAND TIME
10 minutes

1 cup ricotta cheese

1 can (about 4 ounces) mushroom stems and pieces, drained

½ cup refrigerated pesto sauce

8 lasagna noodles, cooked and drained

2 cups Prego® Traditional Italian Sauce *or* Tomato, Basil & Garlic Italian Sauce

¾ cup Pace® Picante Sauce

4 ounces shredded mozzarella cheese (about 1 cup)

1. Stir the ricotta, mushrooms and pesto in a medium bowl. Top **each** noodle with ¼ **cup** of the cheese mixture. Spread to the edges. Roll up like a jelly roll. Place the rolls seam-side down in a 2-quart shallow baking dish.

2. Stir the Italian sauce and picante sauce in a small bowl and pour the mixture over the roll-ups.

3. Bake at 400°F. for 30 minutes or until they're hot and bubbling. Top with the mozzarella cheese. Bake for 5 minutes or until the cheese is melted. Let stand for 10 minutes.

3-Cheese Pasta Bake

Makes 4 servings

1 can (10¾ ounces) Campbell's® Condensed Cream of Mushroom Soup (Regular *or* 98% Fat Free)

1 package (8 ounces) shredded two-cheese blend (about 2 cups)

⅓ cup grated Parmesan cheese

1 cup milk

¼ teaspoon ground black pepper

3 cups corkscrew-shaped pasta (rotini), cooked and drained

1. Stir the soup, cheeses, milk and black pepper in a 1½-quart casserole. Stir in the pasta.

2. Bake at 400°F. for 20 minutes or until the mixture is hot and bubbling.

PREP TIME
20 minutes

BAKE TIME
20 minutes

Kitchen **Tip**

Substitute 2 cups of your favorite shredded cheese for the two-cheese blend.

Hearty Chicken & Noodle Casserole

Makes 4 servings

PREP TIME
15 minutes

BAKE TIME
25 minutes

1 can (10¾ ounces) Campbell's® Condensed Cream of Mushroom Soup (Regular *or* 98% Fat Free)

½ cup milk

1 cup frozen mixed vegetables

2 cups cubed cooked chicken

2 cups medium egg noodles, cooked and drained

¼ cup grated Parmesan cheese

¼ teaspoon ground black pepper

½ cup shredded Cheddar cheese

1. Heat the oven to 400°F. Stir the soup, milk, vegetables, chicken, noodles, Parmesan cheese and black pepper in a 1½-quart casserole.

2. Bake for 25 minutes or until the chicken mixture is hot and bubbling. Stir the chicken mixture. Top with the cheese. Let stand until the cheese is melted.

Kitchen Tip

Easy casseroles like this one are a simple way to transform leftovers. Cooked chicken, turkey or ham will all work in this recipe.

Extra-Easy Spinach Lasagna

Makes 8 servings

1 container (15 ounces) ricotta cheese

1 package (10 ounces) frozen chopped spinach, thawed and well drained

8 ounces shredded mozzarella cheese (about 2 cups)

1 jar (24 ounces) Prego® Fresh Mushroom Italian Sauce

6 *uncooked* lasagna noodles

¼ cup water

1. Stir the ricotta, spinach and **1 cup** mozzarella cheese in a medium bowl.

2. Spread **1 cup** Italian sauce in a 2-quart shallow baking dish. Top with **3** lasagna noodles and **half** the spinach mixture. Repeat the layers. Top with the remaining sauce. Slowly pour water around the inside edges of the baking dish. **Cover.**

3. Bake at 400°F. for 40 minutes. Uncover the dish. Sprinkle with the remaining mozzarella cheese. Bake for 10 minutes or until lasagna is hot and bubbling. Let stand for 10 minutes.

PREP TIME
20 minutes

BAKE TIME
50 minutes

STAND TIME
10 minutes

Kitchen **Tip**

To thaw the spinach, microwave on HIGH for 3 minutes, breaking apart with a fork halfway through heating.

Family Spaghetti Pie

Makes 6 servings

PREP TIME
25 minutes

BAKE TIME
30 minutes

STAND TIME
5 minutes

1 pound ground beef

1 cup Pace® Picante Sauce

1 cup Prego® Fresh Mushroom Italian Sauce

⅓ of a 16-ounce package spaghetti, cooked and drained (about 3 cups)

⅓ cup grated Parmesan cheese

1 egg, beaten

1 tablespoon butter, melted

1 cup ricotta cheese

4 ounces shredded mozzarella cheese (about 1 cup)

1. Cook the beef in a 10-inch skillet over medium-high heat until the beef is well browned, stirring often to separate the meat. Pour off any fat. Stir the picante sauce and Italian sauce into the skillet and cook until hot and bubbling.

2. Stir the spaghetti, Parmesan cheese, egg and butter in a medium bowl. Spread the mixture on the bottom and up the side of a greased 10-inch pie plate. Spread the ricotta in the spaghetti shell. Top with the beef mixture.

3. Bake at 350°F. for 30 minutes or until the mixture is hot and bubbling. Sprinkle with the mozzarella cheese. Let stand for 5 minutes before serving. Cut into **6** wedges.

Easy Pasta Primavera

Makes 4 servings

  2 tablespoons cornstarch

1¾ cups Swanson® Natural Goodness® Chicken Broth

  1 teaspoon dried oregano leaves, crushed

¼ teaspoon garlic powder *or* 2 garlic cloves, minced

  2 cups broccoli florets

  2 medium carrots, sliced (about 1 cup)

  1 medium onion, cut into wedges

  1 medium tomato, diced (about 1 cup)

½ of a 1-pound package thin spaghetti, cooked and drained
     (about 4 cups)

  3 tablespoons grated Parmesan cheese

PREP TIME
20 minutes

COOK TIME
15 minutes

1. Stir the cornstarch and ¾ **cup** broth in a small bowl until the mixture is smooth.

2. Heat the remaining broth, oregano, garlic powder, broccoli, carrots and onion in a 4-quart saucepan over medium heat to a boil. Reduce the heat to low. Cover and cook for 5 minutes or until the vegetables are tender-crisp.

3. Stir the cornstarch mixture in the saucepan. Cook and stir until the mixture boils and thickens. Stir in the tomato. Add the spaghetti and toss to coat. Sprinkle with the cheese.

EASY EVERYDAY MEALS

Baked Macaroni and Cheese

Makes 4 servings

PREP TIME
20 minutes

BAKE TIME
20 minutes

1 can (10¾ ounces) Campbell's® Condensed Cheddar Cheese Soup

½ soup can milk

⅛ teaspoon ground black pepper

2 cups corkscrew-shaped pasta (rotini) *or* shell-shaped pasta, cooked and drained

1 tablespoon dry bread crumbs

2 teaspoons butter, melted

1. Stir the soup, milk, black pepper and pasta in a 1-quart baking dish.

2. Stir the bread crumbs and butter in a small bowl. Sprinkle the bread crumb mixture over the pasta mixture.

3. Bake at 400°F. for 20 minutes or until the pasta mixture is hot and bubbling.

Baked Ziti Supreme

Makes 6 servings

1 pound ground beef

1 medium onion, chopped (about ½ cup)

1 jar (24 ounces) Prego® Fresh Mushroom Italian Sauce

1½ cups shredded mozzarella cheese (6 ounces)

5 cups medium tube-shaped pasta (ziti), cooked and drained

¼ cup grated Parmesan cheese

1. Cook the beef and onion in a 4-quart saucepan over medium-high heat until the beef is well browned, stirring often to separate the meat. Pour off any fat.

2. Stir the Italian sauce, **1 cup** mozzarella cheese and pasta in the saucepan. Spoon the mixture into a 3-quart shallow baking dish. Sprinkle with the remaining mozzarella cheese and Parmesan cheese. Bake at 350°F. for 30 minutes or until hot and bubbling.

PREP TIME
25 minutes

BAKE TIME
30 minutes

Sensational Sides

Country Scalloped Potatoes

Makes 6 servings

PREP TIME
15 minutes

BAKE TIME
1 hour
10 minutes

STAND TIME
10 minutes

1 can (10¾ ounces) Campbell's® Condensed Cream of Celery Soup (Regular *or* 98% Fat Free)

1 can (10½ ounces) Campbell's® Chicken Gravy

1 cup milk

5 medium potatoes, peeled and thinly sliced (about 5 cups)

1 small onion, thinly sliced (about ¼ cup)

2½ cups diced cooked ham

1 cup shredded Cheddar cheese (about 4 ounces)

1. Stir the soup, gravy and milk in a small bowl. Layer **half** the potatoes, onion, ham and soup mixture in a 3-quart shallow baking dish. Repeat the layers. Cover the baking dish.

2. Bake at 375°F. for 40 minutes. Uncover and bake for 25 minutes. Top with the cheese. Bake for 5 minutes or until the potatoes are tender and the cheese is melted. Let stand for 10 minutes.

Cheddar Potato Casserole

Makes 8 servings

PREP TIME
10 minutes

BAKE TIME
30 minutes

Kitchen Tip

*To make
3 cups mashed
potatoes, place
2 pounds
potatoes,
peeled and
cut into 1-inch
pieces, into
a 3-quart
saucepan. Add
water to cover
and heat over
medium-high
heat to a boil.
Reduce the
heat to low.
Cover and cook
for 10 minutes
or until the
potatoes are
tender. Drain.
Mash the
potatoes with
¾ **cup** milk and
2 tablespoons
butter.*

3 cups prepared mashed potatoes

1 can (10¾ ounces) Campbell's® Condensed Cheddar Cheese Soup

⅓ cup sour cream *or* yogurt

Generous dash ground black pepper

1 green onion, chopped (about 2 tablespoons)

1. Stir the potatoes, soup, sour cream, black pepper and onion in a medium bowl. Spoon the potato mixture into a 1½-quart baking dish.

2. Bake at 350°F. for 30 minutes or until the potato mixture is hot.

Bulgur Salad

Makes 6 servings

1¼ cups water

1 cup **uncooked** bulgur wheat

1 cup Pace® Pico De Gallo **or** Pace® Picante Sauce

1 cup rinsed, drained canned black beans

1 cup drained canned whole kernel corn

¼ cup chopped fresh cilantro leaves

1. Heat the water in a 2-quart saucepan over medium-high heat to a boil. Stir the bulgur into the saucepan. Remove the saucepan from the heat. Let stand for 20 minutes.

2. Stir the bulgur, pico de gallo, beans, corn and cilantro in a medium bowl. Serve immediately or cover and refrigerate until ready to serve.

PREP TIME
10 minutes

COOK TIME
5 minutes

STAND TIME
20 minutes

Kitchen **Tip**

For a twist, stir in a squeeze of fresh lime juice.

Green Bean Casserole

Makes 5 servings

PREP TIME
10 minutes

BAKE TIME
30 minutes

1 can (10¾ ounces) Campbell's® Condensed Cream of Mushroom Soup (Regular *or* 98% Fat Free)

½ cup milk

1 teaspoon soy sauce

Dash ground black pepper

2 packages (10 ounces *each*) frozen cut green beans, cooked and drained

1 can (2.8 ounces) French fried onions (1⅓ cups)

Kitchen **Tip**

*You can also make this classic side dish with fresh or canned green beans. You will need either 1½ pounds fresh green beans, cut into 1-inch pieces, cooked and drained, **or** 2 cans (about 16 ounces **each**) cut green beans, drained, for the frozen green beans.*

1. Stir the soup, milk, soy sauce, black pepper, green beans and **⅔ cup** onions in a 1½-quart casserole.

2. Bake at 350°F. for 25 minutes or until hot. Stir the green bean mixture.

3. Sprinkle the remaining onions over the green bean mixture. Bake for 5 minutes more or until onions are golden brown.

Moist & Savory Stuffing

Makes 10 servings

2½ cups Swanson® Chicken Broth (Regular, Natural Goodness® *or* Certified Organic)

Generous dash ground black pepper

2 stalks celery, coarsely chopped (about 1 cup)

1 large onion, coarsely chopped (about 1 cup)

1 package (16 ounces) Pepperidge Farm® Herb Seasoned Stuffing

PREP TIME
10 minutes

COOK TIME
10 minutes

BAKE TIME
30 minutes

Kitchen **Tip**

For crunchier stuffing, bake the casserole uncovered.

1. Heat the broth, black pepper, celery and onion in a 3-quart saucepan over medium-high heat to a boil. Reduce the heat to low. Cover and cook for 5 minutes or until the vegetables are tender, stirring often. Remove the saucepan from the heat. Add the stuffing and mix lightly.

2. Spoon the stuffing mixture into a greased 3-quart shallow baking dish. Cover the baking dish.

3. Bake at 350°F. for 30 minutes or until the stuffing is hot.

Cranberry & Pecan Stuffing: Stir ½ cup **each** dried cranberries **and** chopped pecans into the stuffing mixture.

Sausage & Mushroom Stuffing: Add **1 cup** sliced mushrooms to the vegetables during cooking. Stir ½ **pound** pork sausage, cooked and crumbled, into the stuffing mixture before baking.

Glazed Snow Peas and Carrots

Makes 6 servings

PREP TIME
10 minutes

COOK TIME
20 minutes

4 teaspoons cornstarch

1¾ cups Swanson® Chicken Broth (Regular, Natural Goodness® *or* Certified Organic)

1 teaspoon lemon juice

4 medium carrots, sliced (about 2 cups)

1 medium onion, chopped (about ½ cup)

8 ounces snow peas (about 2 cups)

1. Stir the cornstarch, **½ cup** broth and lemon juice in a small bowl until the mixture is smooth.

2. Stir the remaining broth, carrots and onion in the skillet and heat to a boil. Reduce the heat to low. Cover and cook for 5 minutes or until the vegetables are tender. Stir in the snow peas and cook for 2 minutes.

3. Stir the cornstarch mixture in the skillet. Cook and stir until the mixture boils and thickens.

BLT Salad Toss

Makes 6 servings

½ cup Pace® Picante Sauce

¼ cup prepared Italian salad dressing

6 cups romaine lettuce, torn into bite-sized pieces

2 medium tomatoes, cut into thin wedges

⅔ cup sliced pitted ripe olives

2 cups corn chips

2 ounces shredded Cheddar cheese (about ½ cup)

3 slices bacon, cooked and crumbled

PREP TIME
20 minutes

1. Stir the picante sauce and dressing in a large bowl.

2. Add the lettuce, tomatoes, olives and chips and toss to coat. Top with the cheese and bacon. Serve immediately.

New Potatoes and Peas

Makes 7 servings

PREP TIME
10 minutes

COOK TIME
20 minutes

9 small new potatoes, cut into quarters (about 1½ pounds)

1 can (10¾ ounces) Campbell's® Condensed Cream of Mushroom Soup (Regular *or* 98% Fat Free)

⅓ cup milk

½ teaspoon dried thyme leaves *or* dill weed, crushed

⅛ teaspoon ground black pepper

1 package (10 ounces) frozen peas *or* peas with pearl onions, thawed and drained

1. Place the potatoes in a 4-quart saucepan. Cover the potatoes with water. Heat over high heat to a boil. Reduce the heat to medium. Cook for 8 minutes or until the potatoes are fork-tender. Drain the potatoes in a colander.

2. In the same saucepan, stir the soup, milk, thyme and black pepper. Stir in the potatoes and peas. Heat over low heat, stirring occasionally until heated through.

Savory Vegetables

Makes 4 servings

1 cup Swanson® Chicken Broth (Regular, Natural Goodness® *or* Certified Organic)

3 cups cut-up vegetables*

Use a combination of broccoli florets, cauliflower florets, sliced carrots **and sliced celery.*

1. Heat the broth and vegetables in a 3-quart saucepan over medium-high heat to a boil.

2. Reduce the heat to low. Cover and cook for 5 minutes or until the vegetables are tender-crisp. Drain the vegetables.

PREP TIME
5 minutes

COOK TIME
10 minutes

Desserts

Lemon Cheesecake Tartlets

Makes 24 tarts

THAW TIME
40 minutes

PREP TIME
10 minutes

BAKE TIME
10 minutes

COOL TIME
30 minutes

CHILL TIME
10 minutes

1 package (17.3 ounces) Pepperidge Farm® Frozen Puff Pastry Sheets (2 sheets)

1 egg, beaten

½ of an 8 ounce package cream cheese, softened

½ cup lemon curd

½ cup thawed frozen whipped topping

Fresh raspberries

1. Thaw the pastry sheets at room temperature for 40 minutes or until they're easy to handle. Heat the oven to 375°F. Lightly grease 24 (2½-inch) muffin pan cups.

2. Unfold **1** pastry sheet onto a lightly floured surface. Roll the sheet into a 12×9-inch rectangle. Cut pastry into 12 (3-inch) squares. Press squares into prepared muffin pan cups. Brush top edges of pastry with egg. Repeat with remaining pastry sheet.

3. Bake for 10 minutes or until golden brown. Cool in pans on wire racks for 5 minutes. Remove pastry cups from pans and cool completely on wire racks.

4. Beat the cream cheese in a medium bowl with an electric mixer on medium speed until it's smooth. Beat in the lemon curd. Stir in the whipped topping.

5. Spoon about **1 tablespoon** cheese mixture into each pastry cup. Refrigerate for at least 10 minutes before serving, up to 1 day ahead. Top with a raspberry.

Tomato Soup Spice Cake

Makes 12 servings

PREP TIME
20 minutes

BAKE TIME
40 minutes

COOL TIME
20 minutes

2 cups all-purpose flour

1⅓ cups sugar

4 teaspoons baking powder

1½ teaspoons ground allspice

1 teaspoon baking soda

1 teaspoon ground cinnamon

½ teaspoon ground cloves

1 can (10¾ ounces) Campbell's® Condensed Tomato Soup

½ cup vegetable shortening

2 eggs

¼ cup water

Cream Cheese Frosting

Kitchen **Tip**

The cake can also be prepared in a 13×9-inch baking pan.

1. Heat the oven to 350°F. Grease **2** (8- or 9-inch) cake pans.

2. Stir the flour, sugar, baking powder, allspice, baking soda, cinnamon and cloves in a large bowl. Add the soup, shortening, eggs and water. Beat with an electric mixer on low speed just until blended. Increase the speed to high and beat for 4 minutes. Pour the batter into the pans.

3. Bake for 40 minutes or until a toothpick inserted in the centers comes out clean. Let the cakes cool in the pans on wire racks for 20 minutes. Frost with the *Cream Cheese Frosting*.

Cream Cheese Frosting: Beat **1 package** (8 ounces) cream cheese, softened, **2 tablespoons** milk and **1 teaspoon** vanilla extract in a medium bowl with an electric mixer on medium speed until the mixture is creamy. Slowly beat in **1 package** (16 ounces) confectioners' sugar until the frosting is desired consistency.

Chocolate Goldfish® Pretzel Clusters

Makes 24 servings

1 package (12 ounces) semi-sweet chocolate pieces (about 2 cups)
2½ cups Pepperidge Farm® Pretzel Goldfish® Crackers
1 container (4 ounces) multi-colored nonpareils

1. Line a baking sheet with wax paper.

2. Place the chocolate into a microwavable bowl. Microwave on MEDIUM for 30 seconds. Stir. Repeat until the chocolate is melted and smooth. Add the Goldfish® crackers and stir to coat.

3. Drop the chocolate mixture by tablespoonfuls onto the baking sheet. Sprinkle the clusters with the nonpareils.

4. Refrigerate for 30 minutes or until the clusters are firm. Keep refrigerated until ready to serve.

PREP TIME
5 minutes

COOK TIME
1 minute

CHILL TIME
30 minutes

Kitchen **Tip**

To wrap for gift-giving, arrange the clusters in a small box lined with colored plastic wrap.

Chocolate-Cinnamon Bread Pudding

Makes 6 servings

PREP TIME
15 minutes

BAKE TIME
40 minutes

Kitchen **Tip**

This bread pudding can be served with the whipped cream as a dessert, or with a sprinkle of confectioners' sugar as a decadent brunch dish.

12 slices Pepperidge Farm® Cinnamon Swirl Bread, any variety, cut into cubes (about 6 cups)

½ cup semi-sweet chocolate pieces

2½ cups milk

4 eggs

½ cup packed brown sugar

1 teaspoon vanilla extract

Sweetened whipped cream (optional)

1. Heat the oven to 350°F.

2. Place the bread cubes into a lightly greased 2-quart shallow baking dish. Sprinkle the chocolate pieces over the bread cubes. Beat the milk, eggs, brown sugar and vanilla extract in a small bowl with a fork or whisk. Pour the milk mixture over the bread cubes. Stir and press the bread cubes into the milk mixture to coat.

3. Bake for 40 minutes or until a knife inserted in the center comes out clean. Serve with the whipped cream, if desired.

Berry Bordeaux Desserts

Makes 12 servings

24 **Pepperidge Farm® Bordeaux® Cookies**

1 **cup heavy cream**

¼ **cup sugar**

1 **teaspoon vanilla extract**

3 **cups mixed berries***

Mint leaves (optional)

Use a combination of sliced strawberries, raspberries, blackberries **and blueberries.*

PREP TIME
20 minutes

CHILL TIME
3 hours

1. Place **12** cookies into a 2-quart shallow baking dish.

2. Beat the heavy cream, **2 tablespoons** sugar and vanilla extract in a medium bowl with an electric mixer on high speed until stiff peaks form.

3. Spoon the whipped cream in the baking dish. Top with the remaining cookies. Cover and refrigerate for 3 hours or until the cookies are soft.

4. Stir the berries with the remaining sugar in a medium bowl. Spoon the berry mixture over the cookie mixture. Garnish with the mint, if desired.

Puff Pastry Chocolatines

Makes 12 servings

PREP TIME
1 hour

BAKE TIME
15 minutes

COOL TIME
10 minutes

½ of a 17.3-ounce package Pepperidge Farm® Puff Pastry Sheets (1 sheet), thawed

1 egg, beaten

8 bars (1.5 ounces *each*) milk *or* dark chocolate, chopped

Confectioners' sugar

1. Heat the oven to 375°F.

2. Unfold the pastry sheet on a lightly floured surface. Cut the pastry sheet into **12** (3×2½-inch) rectangles. With a short side facing you, brush the top third of **each** rectangle with the egg. Place **about 1 tablespoon** chocolate in the center of **each** rectangle. Starting at the short end closest to you, roll up like a jelly roll. Place the filled pastries onto a baking sheet. Brush with the egg.

3. Bake for 15 minutes or until the pastries are golden brown. Remove the pastries from the baking sheet and let cool on a wire rack for 10 minutes. Sprinkle the pastries with the confectioners' sugar.

Cranberry-Walnut Crostadas

Makes 6 servings

1 package (10 ounces) Pepperidge Farm® Puff Pastry Shells

1 cup heavy cream

¼ cup sugar

1½ cups toasted walnut halves, chopped

1 cup dried cranberries

¼ teaspoon ground cinnamon

   Assorted Toppings

PREP TIME
20 minutes

COOK TIME
10 minutes

COOL TIME
20 minutes

1. Prepare the pastry shells according to the package directions.

2. Heat the heavy cream and sugar in a 1-quart heavy saucepan over medium heat to a boil. Cook for 5 minutes or until the mixture is thickened, stirring occasionally. Remove the saucepan from the heat. Let the mixture cool to room temperature. Stir in the walnuts, cranberries and cinnamon.

3. Divide the walnut mixture among the pastry shells. Top the filled shells with one of the *Assorted Toppings*, if desired.

Assorted Toppings: Almond-flavored **or** orange-flavored liqueur-sweetened whipped cream, crumbled Roquefort **or** other bleu cheese, wedges of Cheddar cheese.

Index